Is It Just My Imagination?

Utilizing Your God-Given Imagination

Ternae T. Jordan Jr.

IS IT JUST MY IMAGINATION.
©2015 Miraclechild Media Group, Inc.

Unless otherwise indicated, all Scripture quotations are taken from the New International Version.

ISBN 978-0-692-45126-7

Edited By: Beverly Sonnier

Headshot & Cover Design: MS Design and Photography

For Booking: booking@miraclechildmediagroup.com

Email: info@miraclechildmediagroup.com

www.miraclechildmediagroup.com

www.ternaejordan.com

This book is dedicated to my daughter,
Deanna Katrina Jordan.

Follow your dreams as God leads you.
Daddy loves you!

Acknowledgements

Words alone cannot convey the heartfelt gratitude I hold for the people who have influenced me for the better on this incredible journey, especially my family who supported, loved and encouraged me along the way.

To my wife, Demetria. Thank you for your encouragement and support! Your love, patience, and prayers are what motivate me. You are a dream come true. As I dream, I dream with you in mind. I Love You!

To my parents, Dr. Ternae and Angela Jordan. Thank you for allowing me to freely dream and for exposing me to a world outside of a box. Your support, encouragement, and belief in the desires of my heart are what give me the confidence and drive to reach beyond what I can physically see and accomplish my dreams. I Love You!

To my sister, DeJuan. Thank you for being you! You believed in my gifts when I didn't! Thank you for encouraging, supporting, loving and believing in me and my dreams! I Love You.

To my brother, JaMichael. Thank you Bro! I thank you for pushing and challenging me to become better! I am a better man because you did not see me any other way. I Love You!

Finally, I thank God for all things, great and small. To GOD be the glory...

Contents

Foreword

Title: *"Is It Just My Imagination?" (Utilizing your God-Given Imagination)*
By: Tommy Ford

I have always known that God had a plan for my life. Though I had no idea what those plans were, I did believe that it transcended the mentality of many of my peers, people in my community, culture and family. I've always had a wild imagination and my imagination truly serves me well in my career. I've been blessed to have experienced and witness how my imagination has assisted my dreams into becoming a reality. This power of imagination also has a way of attracting other people with the same gift. I've been blessed to work with some of the most successful, creative and talented individuals who have allowed their imaginations to create for themselves successful careers. God has used these relationships to fuel, challenge and encourage me to push my imagination to the limit, which has made me a better actor, father and businessman.

I worked five seasons on the syndicated show "Martin", however the show has been on air all over the world for more than twenty years! I can't even explain how much my imagination has been stretched by working with actors such as Martin Lawrence, Tisha Campbell, Tichina Arnold, Carl Anthony Payne II and many other great actors and actresses. The imagination that these individuals' possess is what made the show so exciting and successful. Not to mention other shows and movies that I've been blessed to have appeared in, such as Harlem Nights, Law and Order, New York Undercover, The Parkers and tons more, but they all had to be scripted, produced and acted out through active imaginations.

I am often asked, "Were members of your family in show business? Is that how you ended up in entertainment?" The answer is no. No one in my family has ever acted before. The possibility of a successful career in show business was birthed in my imagination (I'M-A-GIANT-NATION)!

Although my family had not introduced me to acting, they did introduce me to Christ! As result of being in Christ...I learned that *I can do all things* **(that I imagine)** through Christ who gives me strength! YES, I've had many odds against me, but it was utilizing my God-Given imagination that helped me to overcome them. As a child I learned that if I *delight myself in the Lord*, that He promised to give me the *desires of my heart!* What's in my heart? My heart was filled with imaginations! Imaginations of getting out of: the ghetto; poverty; ignorance; crime; addictions and the hopelessness of generational curses!

In this book, "Is It Just My Imagination", Ternae Jordan, Jr., gives us, the reader, powerful tools to help stretch our imaginations and accomplish our dreams, goals and God's will for our lives and His Kingdom. I believe that it was God's gift of imagination that birthed this book in Ternae's spirit, and it was Ternae's imagination that brought us together.

Several years ago, I accepted a speaking engagement in Chattanooga, Tennessee, with the purpose of speaking and encouraging students in several inner-city schools, churches and the community. It was during this trip that I met Ternae, who was actively working with youth in the schools through a nonprofit organization called Stop the Madness National, Inc. I had no idea that I would meet this young man!

During that time, I was producing and working on various film projects and asked him if he would look at a project that I was working on and he obliged. I pulled out my laptop and showed him two short films that I produced. After Ternae viewed the film, he asked me if I had ever thought of writing a faith-based film? At that time I told him that it had never crossed my mind. Ternae began to share with me his heart and his miraculous testimony, which led him to starting his company, Miraclechild Media Group, Inc. He shared how God wanted him to share the Gospel with the world, through the various forms of media and specifically through film and music, and how his efforts to reach out to other faith-based film and record companies for help, was met with rejection. It was during this conversation that I saw his passion, heard his dreams and witnessed his imagination at work. What Ternae didn't know is that the whole time he was speaking, it was as if I saw and heard myself speaking through him! I recognized his passion, his spirit, his heart, but most importantly...his IMAGINATION! God spoke to me at that moment and told me that Ternae and

I will work together in some capacity! My imagination recognized his imagination and it caused a reaction, and it forced me to respond! IMAGINE THAT!

I know that this book will encourage you, challenge you and stretch you, but if you take heed, pray and apply the tools that Ternae teaches to your life, I believe that your imagination will take your life to a place that's unimaginable.

Because of the character I play on Martin, I'm often asked if I have a job. I always say..."Yes...absolutely! My job is to be about my Father's business!" I believe that our job is to use our God – Given Imaginations to build the body of Christ! Our powerful imaginations will lead us toward an abundant life with and for Christ Jesus!

YOU'VE GOTTA JOB DAWG

Tommy Ford

Foreword

By: Scott Maclellan

This book will open your mind to the world of possibilities and the endless depth of your potential. I was blown away by the simple yet profound words written in this book.

The many revelations that are revealed throughout this book are simply amazing and captivating. You will be astonished by the capabilities you have by simply utilizing your imagination in ways like never before. You will be challenged to think outside the box and you will be pushed to greater levels of thinking. God has equipped all of us with an imagination but sometimes life circumstances causes us to stop using our imagination. We may even begin to think it is child-like to do so. However, this book will give you the tools you need to start dreaming again and imagine what is possible. Your life will be renewed through this transformation of your mind. Your entire thought process will be given a makeover.

Some of the surprising facts about this book are the

answers to some of life's simple questions. I found myself reflecting and pondering the God given power of my imagination and the impact it has on my life. I can say without a shadow of a doubt that a substantial amount of intellect and research was put into this book.

Scott Maclellan

Maclellan Foundation, Inc.

Prologue

He was only 15 years old and had always dreamed and imagined himself being a songwriter, music producer, and entertainer who would perform on stages around the world, while people screamed his name as it was illuminated in lights. He knew that to accomplish this dream he would have to learn the craft of music, so his parents signed he and his younger sister up for piano lessons. After each piano lesson, this young boy, filled with enthusiasm and excitement, rushed home to put what he had learned into practice. He began to write song after song, recording them on an old raggedy tape recorder to play for family and friends. With each lesson his song writing skills improved, his singing got better, and his passion for music grew stronger. He was well on his way to accomplishing his dreams.

On October 27, 1993, following their weekly piano lesson, the siblings did exactly what their parents told them to do, they sat on the couch in the lobby, in front of the big picture window and waited for their mother to pick them up. While waiting, the young boy went over in his head what his piano instructor told him to practice. Suddenly, a fight broke out between two boys and the center employee told the boys to take their altercation outside. Moments later, gunshots rang out and the center employees ran to lock the doors to keep the danger outside and those inside safe. People began running for cover, when suddenly two of those bullets entered into the community center through the big picture window, with a bullet lodging into a wall. Suddenly, the 15 year old aspiring musician heard a loud ringing in his right ear, his head began to feel as if it was vibrating, everyone appeared to be moving in slow motion, and his entire body began to get hot. Suddenly someone yelled, "That boy got shot in the head!" It wasn't until that life altering announcement and the bone chilling screams of his younger sister, that the young boy realized that the second bullet had landed in his head. Still alert, the young boy began crying, praying and repeatedly saying, "I'm going to die. Lord, I don't want to die."

Sadly, the young boy died on the floor of that community center while in pursuit of his dreams. He was an innocent bystander, in a safe haven for young people, trying to prepare for a desired dream and

goal that he had imagined for his life. Tragical-
ly, there are many young people who will never see
their dreams become a reality, due to senseless violence and other forms of madness that are present in
the world. This young boy was a good kid, he didn't
have enemies, he loved the Lord, and he was obedient to God as well as his parents.

Let me pose to you this question. Would you continue to follow your dreams, even if your life depended
on it? Maybe you feel like your dreams have already
died and they can't be revived. There is much that
God wants to reveal to you through this young boy's
life. We have to remember that there is a "test" in
every testimony and this young boy and his family
were truly tested.

Fortunately, through the prayers of those standing
around and the quick response of the paramedics,
the young boy was revived and rushed to the hospital where he continued to fight for his life. The doctors desperately continued to work on him. The line
on the device that monitored his heart began to go
from a jagged line to a straight line and the chanc-
es of his life being saved looked bleak. The doctors

feared the worst. Although, they had succeeded in reviving him, his parents were told that "IF" he lived, he would likely be in a vegetative state for the rest of his life; blind, unable to walk, and with complete loss and function of his motor skills. BUT GOD!

Through the faith and prayers of those in the community, the professional and proficient work of the doctors, they were able to stabilize the young boy's condition. I'm not telling you what I heard; I am telling you what I know. I know that God worked a miracle in that teenager's life, because the young boy that was shot in the head at age 15 was me, and this is MY testimony. I thank God for saving my life and for this reason I know that God continues to be a healer and work miracles today.

I could very well end the story here, but I can't. There's more that I need to share with you—to encourage you. Every word that is written in this book has been burning in my spirit for over 10 years. I am very passionate in seeing God's people flourish and prosper in the promises of God. Especially you!

Introduction

If they'd dared come into our home, they'd better have come in with a hope and a prayer, because they would not have left the house the way they came in. Oh, how battered and bruised they would have been after I was done with them. I can imagine how that special report on the six o'clock news would have gone that evening: "A ten year old boy saved his family's life from burglars as he defended them with his weapons of Kung Fu, Karate, and Jujitsu". There was no way that I was going to let thieves break into my parents' home and harm my mother, father, sister and brother–not if I had something to do with it. Did I know martial arts? No. Had I beaten up thieves before? No way. Did I suddenly wake up that morning with the knowledge and gift of a tenth degree black belt? Why, of course not.

Ok, ok. I admit, if burglars would have broken into our home to harm my family and I, there was not much that I could have done, other than run and find a hiding place and pray that God would protect us. I know that it was a ridiculous thought for a ten-year-old boy to have, but it wasn't ridiculous to me.

Every Sunday morning while waiting for my mother to get ready and take us to church, I would sit in the living room dressed in my Sunday best repeatedly watching Kung Fu movies. It seems like it was only yesterday that I playfully kicked and punched my little sister during each commercial break, mimicking the moves I saw on TV, just to prove to her and convince myself that I was just as good as the fighters on television. Of course I didn't have the knowledge or gift of a tenth degree black belt, nor was I a Ninja, boxer, or wrestler. However, my imagination was so strong that I mentally convinced myself that I was a great fighter and that I could protect not only my family, but the world as well. Yes, it was ridiculous when I think back on it, and my wild imagination could get a little out of hand.

Actually, if you're really honest with yourself, you can probably remember during your childhood when you, too, had an imagination that convinced you of things that weren't so. Perhaps you were that child who thought you had superman or superwoman powers; Tucking an old dingy t-shirt into the back of the shirt you were wearing and pretending the shirt was a superhero's cape. Then you would extend your arms out in front of you while running around the house. In your mind you were a super-hero and you were flying through the air. Or maybe you were like my little sister, placing that same old dingy t-shirt on your head and letting it hang down pretending to have long hair like a supermodel or TV actress. Perhaps, you were that little boy who imagined being a professional football, basketball or baseball player, or just maybe you were that little girl who walked around in her mother's heels or snuck into her mother's room to get a sneak peek of what you looked like in her make up before she caught you. Honestly, I don't know who you were when your imagination took over, but one thing I am almost sure of, IT WAS ALL REAL TO YOU!

Yes, this is the greatest thing about our imagination. Our imagination is so powerful, that when we think about how we have failed to use it, we realize that our lives could have been much better if we had used it properly. Perhaps we would have made better choices, set better goals, we would have married a different person or graduated from high school or college. Maybe we wouldn't have had to serve that prison sentence, we would have better health, but most of all, maybe we would be living our dreams. You know, the dreams you had before "life happened."

The imagination of a child is one of the God's greatest gifts. Unfortunately, our youth have been polluted and tainted by this world, destroying their imagination. Unlike some of us, many young people do not get to experience the full potential and enjoyment of their imagination. Today, because of factors such as: fatherless homes, domestic violence, child abuse, neglect, poverty, gangs, drugs, teenage pregnancies, divorce, and many other factors, our youth have been mentally paralyzed. In addition, our young people have been desensitized by the media and by certain types of music. The imagination of people of all ages is being tampered with and diluted through Satan's deceptions and schemes, which has left our imaginations exhausted and almost nonexistent. Without an active imagination, we have NOTHING!

The twin sister to imagination is VISION. Imagination and vision never leave each other's side. The word of God says, "Where there is no vision, the people perish" (Prov. 29:18). This is so true. So many of God's children are being destroyed and are going to their graves prematurely because they lack vision or have lost sight of their vision. It has to be understood that within imagination lays vision, hope, happiness, joy, promise, and purpose.

This book was written to encourage and challenge you to use the imagination that God has given you to fulfill not only your dreams, but God's desires for you, as well. The Bible tells us in Genesis 1:26 that God said, "Let us make man in our image, in our likeness." He then goes on to say in verse 27, "So God created man in his own image, in the image of God he created him; male and female he created them." So, if God created us like himself, shouldn't we have the characteristics of GOD? Of course we should.

Not only did God create us, he created light, seas, mountains, trees, animals, seasons, day and night, clouds, the sky, snow, rain, stars, and vegetation; He created everything.

We can agree that God's creations and his way of creating them is remarkable. Especially, in the way that He strategically manufactured our bodies. Just look at the way our organs function and operate with each other; the way the veins connect to one another to keep blood running through our bodies. Think about the way our limbs collaborate to perform a specific task. When we think about all of the things that God created and how they work, we can agree that it had to take an AMAZING IMAGI-NATION to accomplish such. If God can imagine a world, such as this and simply speak it into existence, then shouldn't we have that same authority if we are made in his image and likeness? Yes, we should.

While reading this book, you will see the power of the imagination and how it aligns with your faith. Just like faith, our imagination is irrelevant without works (James 2:20). We can imagine a better life, wealth, health, happiness, a healed marriage, a new job or career, a new home or automobile, friends, love, or anything else you desire, but if your imagination isn't fueled and ignited with action, excitement, joy, energy, and a thrust of hope, that fire will soon burn out.

In order to get the most out of this book, you will

have to clear your mind of all that troubles you, including stress and doubt. Remember, faith is the substance of things hoped for and the evidence of things not seen (Hebrews 1:1). Imagination is the vision of what could be, but is not physically seen... yet.

You will have to use your imagination to get what God wants you to get from every page of this book. Try to tap into that long lost child-like imagination and imagine the things that were bazaar to others but real to you. Imagination is real and it never grows old, but it can die if it doesn't have a reason to live. If your imagination has died, let's revive it. If it's lost, let's find it. Are you ready? Good! So am I.

1

The Importance Of Imagination

> "There is a treasure within you that must come out. Don't go to the grave with your treasure still within you."
>
> –Dr. Myles Munroe

Life has a very unique way of distracting us from utilizing the tools God has given us to use for an enjoyable and prosperous life. We are often so busy that we can't find time to imagine our life without that stressful nine to five, without arguments with our spouse, without disagreements with the children, co-workers, and the boss; or without those nagging negative situations that sneak up on us like a dangerous criminal in the dark. Is it possible that you are so busy that you have allowed negative and dysfunctional situations and circumstances to convince you that this is just how it is, so you should just be thankful and content because it could be worse?

If you answered yes to either of these questions, guess what? You are not alone. Far too many people feel this way and have allowed great things and opportunities in life to pass them by. Satan wants to discredit your imagination and make you feel as if imagining anything better for yourself is nothing but childish and foolish thinking. If Satan has enticed your mind with these thoughts, let me encourage and remind you that there is nothing childish about using your imagination and allowing it to bring peace, comfort, and happiness to your life. As a matter of fact, God has allowed people to use His gift of imagination to create so much for you and your loved ones to enjoy. Without an imagination there would be no getaway vacations with five star hotels to rest in, no airplanes to travel the world, no automobiles to travel from point A to point B, no movies or movie theaters, computers, televisions, great books to read, jobs or careers, and so on. The things you love to do, and the things that make you happy were all birthed through someone's imagination, whether through God's imagination or man's.

The greatest part of all of this is that the imagination never dies; but it can become incapacitated from the lack of use. An incapacitated imagination leads to loss of creativity and unfulfilled potential. The late Dr. Myles Munroe, a great leader and visionary, once said, "The wealthiest places in the world are not gold mines, oil fields, diamond mines or banks. The wealthiest place is the cemetery. There lies companies that were never started, masterpieces that were never painted... In the cemetery there is buried the greatest treasure of untapped potential. There is a treasure within you that must come out. Don't go to the grave with your treasure still within YOU." Dr. Munroe also said, "You must decide if you are going to rob the world or bless it with the rich, valuable, potent, untapped resources locked away within you." I have always believed these statements held so much truth. Six feet underneath numerous tombstones lay corpses that once had living and active minds that held great imaginations that never went further than a thought. I'm very sure that many of these imaginations could have come up with a cure for terminal and debilitating diseases; or could have provided a solution to end poverty, wars, homelessness and so much more. Unfortunately, like many of us, they allowed Satan to discourage them and make a mockery of their thoughts and visions. So they left this world without seeing what they could have been or could have done if they had only allowed what they imagined become a reality. Reality, you ask? Yes, reality. Our imaginations can become a reality if we truly believe in it and in what we have imagined and put our faith in God the Father who gives it. We must also put to work what we imagine. Faith without works is dead (James 2:26) and so is imagination.

God created the universe and everything in it in six days. The things He created are so detailed and purposeful that it had to take an amazing imagination to see what He saw. It also had to take considerable faith to speak it into existence and know with confidence that it was all good. After God imagined it, He spoke it, or let's say created it. God had to make sure that His creation prospered and flourished. So what did He do? God created a man and He named him Adam. God's command to Adam was to work and cultivate what He had created through His imagination. God left Adam in charge to make sure all that He imagined and created was nurtured and protected, which also means that we have to protect our imagination. We have to protect what we imagine simply because it is a gift from God. Imaginations are also very powerful and can be influential and important in many things for this world. Let's review how God worked His imagination

1. God Imagined It:

"In the beginning God created the heavens and the earth. And the earth was without form, and void: and darkness was upon the face of the deep" (Gen. 1: 1-2). This Scripture demonstrates that before God created anything there was "nothing." The earth and the heavens were without form. At the beginning of it all, God had a blank canvas with no picture or image. The only image God could have had was the image He imagined. God saw the darkness and knew that the beautiful things that He was imagining needed to be seen. So He created light. Genesis 1:3-4 says, "And God said, 'Let there be light,' and there was light. And God saw the light that it was good, and God divided the light from the darkness."

Similarly, we have to turn on the light in our mind. That light is the beginning of illumination of confidence for what is about to happen. Without light, nothing you imagine will matter if you cannot see it. Light has to be turned on in your mind to help you see that your imagination is not just a fairy tale, but reality being unleashed. When the light of belief is turned on, you will be able to clearly see the truth behind all that you imagine. Light is **belief** and darkness is **doubt**. Just as God separated the light from darkness, allow Him to separate your belief from your doubt. Just as light and darkness do not mix, neither does doubt and belief.

After God created the universe and everything in it, He looked at it and saw that it was good. God was very pleased with the results of what His imagination had created. However, God's imagination did not end with the creation of light. It was still working. God created the universe and earth and everything thereof, but He had one more thing that He needed to create.

God was imagining a masterpiece, and what He had in mind was going to be so special to Him that He didn't just want to speak it into existence like everything else. God wanted to personally mold this creation with His very own hands. It was so important that He asked for the counsel of three to assist:

"Then God said, 'Let Us make man in Our image, after Our likeness....'" (Gen. 1: 26).

This masterpiece was so significant that he said "Let (Us) make man in (Our) own Image." We were so important to God that he decided to have the Son (Jesus) and the Holy Spirit help Him create us. Wow! God thought that much of us that He spent extra time on us. He molded man and woman with His very own hands and breathed the breath of life into their nostrils. You and I are descendants of this creation, which means we are all made in God's image and His likeness. God created by first imagining it then speaking it. And it all came into existence.

2. He Spoke It Into Existence:

God had the authority to speak it, and it came to pass. God has given us all the same authority. We have to be confident that if God places a vision in us He will give us the provision to see it through. We just have to take authority over that which God has given us, speak it by faith, and believe it will be done.

Proverbs 18:21 tells us that, *"Death and life are in the power of the tongue, and they that love it shall eat the fruits thereof."* We have the option to speak *life* to what we imagine or speak *death*. I am positive that God would not have said, *"Let there be"* if He did not believe it would become. God had so much authority and belief in what He imagined that He confidently spoke it into existence, and everything He imagined came to pass. These things were night, day, the oceans, land, the stars, trees, the mountains, fruits and vegetables, the sky, animals, you, I and everything else within this earth and the Universe.

In that same way we should speak positively and confidently regarding what we believe and follow Habakkuk 2: 2-3, which reads, *"Write the vision, and make it plain upon tables, that he may run that readeth it. For the vision is yet for an appointed time, but at the end it shall speak and not lie: though it tarry, wait for it; because it will surely come, it will not tarry."*

Write your vision down on paper or create that business plan. Surround yourself with people who have already had what they've imagined become reality. Be mindful that it may not come to light (pass) immediately or when you want it to, but keep believing and speaking it. You have to be confident in your imagination and you have to speak with authority regarding it. You will discover over time that you inspire others to believe in their imagination as well.

3. God Worked It.

Thirdly, God used Adam and Eve to work the vision. He gave them a plan and blueprint of how to keep what He imagined alive, and He gave them the opportunity to enjoy it themselves. However, the benefits Adam and Eve experienced were short lived because they disobeyed God's command and committed sin in His eyes. Sadly, this is also the case for many believers. Many of us have great imaginations. We believe in what we imagine and we speak it into existence and it becomes reality, but the reality is short lived due to our sinful nature. Sin and a prosperous imagination does not work well together. It may work for a while, but it does not last.

As an example, let's say a Fortune 500 company made billions of dollars over the course of a year. The business consistently grew financially. The CEO, investors, employees, and everyone involved in making the business successful, prospered financially because of someone's imagination. That person imagined it, he or she believed in it, and then he or she spoke it into existence. However, it came to pass only when they did the work. They likely made presentations and submitted proposals to investors and loan officers. Regardless of what they had to do, they put into action what they imagined and worked the vision.

Now, let's look at another example of a Fortune 500 company. Over the course of a year, this successful company made billions of dollars. However, the CEO and employees stole, embezzled money, plotted schemes, deceived people, and lied. Due to their sinful behavior, the company eventually folded. You see, it is equally important to have the right people working your vision. Your imagination and your vision are valuable and you have to protect it.

There are billions of people around the world with an abundance of imagination. Yours isn't the only one that exists. Everyone has one. However, you are the only one who has YOUR imagination. You may imagine some of the same things as your neighbor next door, the man thousands of miles away, the girl down the street or the woman at work, but what you imagine is still not the same as what they imagine. There are details in what you imagine that do not appear in what another person imagines. That is why your imagination is unique. You own it, God gave it to you, and you are responsible for how it is used; so don't waste it. Learn how to believe in it. Learn how to use it, and use it properly. Use it the way God intended it to be used and it will drastically guide and or change your life for the better! A great imagination is a terrible thing to waste.

2

Protected

> "Limitations live only in our minds, but if we use our imaginations, our possibilities become limitless."
>
> **–Jamie Paolinetti**

Growing up as a pastor's kid had its advantages and disadvantages. I must admit, I love God and I love praising his name, but as a child, I really didn't like the long drawn out Sunday morning and evening services. I grew even more tired of the Wednesday night Bible studies, the Thursday night choir rehearsals, and the Saturday morning rehearsals for the children's choir and junior usher board meetings. I definitely did not look forward to Easter and Christmas speech rehearsals, church anniversary celebrations, pastor anniversary celebrations, or the countless other church events.. To be honest, church just wasn't my cup of tea, and if I could have had it my way, I would have preferred to stay at home singing "Kumbayah" or "Jesus Loves Me."

Unfortunately, my opinions and ideas about a more
exciting and fun filled church experience for a kid
didn't mean a hill of beans to my parents. So, I
grudgingly participated in various church events,
simply because my parents dragged me to church
with them and made me participate. Besides, it
didn't look good for the Pastor, who was also my
father, to ask his congregation to bring their children to participate in church activities while his
own children were at home watching television or
outside playing with the neighborhood children.
Nevertheless, there we were, my siblings and I, par-
ticipating in just about every ministry and activity
that the church offered.

I did, however, love the privileges that being a part of
the first family offered, such as being first in line to
eat the savory soul food that the ladies of the church
prepared for special events; or enjoying the kindness
of the church members who were always there to
help and bless our family with whatever we might
need–deacons, mothers of the church, and sometimes even strangers were always there to show their
love for our family. Most of all, I loved the gifts that
members of the congregation would present to my

family on special occasions. Yes, we received many gifts from many people.

In my mind, some gifts were great and some were not so great, but my parents were always grateful for any gift they received. I remember one particular time when I received a gift that disappointed me. I was thankful, but I wasn't excited about the gift. My mother said to me, "TJ, I know you're not happy about this gift, but it is a gift that someone wanted to give you, so you have to protect and cherish it."

When I think back to that day, I can honestly say that I was being a little selfish and inconsiderate regarding the gift. I did not take into consideration the fact that maybe the person who gave it to me wasn't able to afford anything better, and that they gave it from their heart. Maybe they really thought I would like that particular gift based upon their perception of me. Whatever the case, maybe my role as the receiver was to accept the gift, protect it and cherish it. Our imaginations are like those gifts. They are truly gifts from God, and because of that, we must cherish and protect our imaginations, as well.

To protect means to defend or guard from attack, invasion, loss, annoyance, insult, etc. to cover or shield from injury or danger *(dictionary.com)*. As recipients of the gift, it is our job and duty to protect, guard, and cover our imaginations from the attacks of the enemy. Satan knows, that if he destroys our imagination, he can put an end to the purpose that God has for our lives.

Jamie Paolinetti, an experienced journeymen in American cycling, filmmaker and writer said, "Limitations live only in our minds, but if we use our imaginations, our possibilities become limitless." Our imaginations are limitless. This reminds me of a statement that I have heard all of my life. "The sky is the limit!" Ok, sounds good. I've heard it hundreds of times, but never really understood it until I got older. You see there has never been anyone who has been able to measure the sky. There isn't any accurate measurement of how wide or tall the sky is. No one knows, and we may never find out. If the sky is the limit and no one can tell us its measurements, thus it becomes limitless. So are our imagination and potential. Who can tell us what we can or cannot do?

There is no one in this world—past, present or future that can limit the scope of what we can imagine. We are what we think. If we think we can, we can; if we think we can't, then guess what, we can't. The little engine that could did so because he knew he could.

"As a man thinketh in his heart so is he" (Prov. 23:7). We have to understand that there is no way we can think with that blood-pumping organ behind our rib cage called the *heart.* So what heart is this Scripture referring to? It's referring to the heart of man— *the mind.* The mind is where the imagination lives, feeds, and grows. When we think limitlessly, there is no limit to our imagination and what we can accomplish by doing the work.

Albert Einstein, a wise scientist said, "Imagination is more important than knowledge. For knowledge is limited to all we now know and understand, while imagination embraces the entire world, and all there ever will be to know and understand." Again, our imaginations are limitless. It is good to gain knowledge and understanding, but without imagination we will limit what we know, learn, and understand.

There is so much in this world that we don't know, but using our imagination can help us figure out some things that are currently unknown.

I remember during my elementary years and part of my middle school years that every progress report and report card sent home to my parents had a little note attached to it for them that read something like, "Ternae is a wonderful student and has great potential to improve academically, if only he didn't *daydream* so much in class." They received this message so much that I began to believe that "daydreaming" was a negative thing.

Daydreaming is defined as a "visionary fantasy." Daydreaming happens to the best of us. It is that moment when you find yourself engaged in pleasant, happy, peaceful fantasies or thoughts while becoming detached from your present reality and surroundings. Daydreaming helps us to generate new ideas and imagine things that are seemingly impossible. This could actually be a good thing when you find yourself suffocating from negative surroundings and you need to use your God-given imagination to momentarily relocate to a peaceful place. It can however, become a negative thing if we allow it to distract us from things of importance or places us in dangerous situations, such as burning your food on the stove or causing a car accident because you were daydreaming and ran a red light.. I do believe however, that if daydreaming is done properly, it has the power to ignite a fire within a person that could positively alter their lives forever.

God gave us our imaginations before our mothers and fathers ever laid eyes on us and held us in their arms. Before parents ever hear the cries of their newborn babies, their imaginations are already at work. It has been researched and documented that a 32-week old fetus, is able to feel and dream. Re-searchers speculate that fetuses dream about what they know, the sensations they feel, what they hear, taste and smell. Fetuses dream about whatever the environment teaches them.

Have you ever wondered about if blind people dream? And if they do dream can they see their dreams? Many people have asked these questions. Research has shown that everyone dreams. Isn't that just like God not to exclude anyone from hav-ing the ability to dream?

Dreaming is a gift to everyone regardless of his or her ailment, circumstance, or situation. People born blind will not dream visual dreams, as people who have sight. They will dream about what their environment teaches them. Like fetuses, they will dream about what they hear, taste, smell, and feel. Some individuals who are not 100 percent blind can see blurred objects, so that's what they dream. If they see silhouettes, then they dream silhouette images. An individual's environment and the events within it dictate how he or she dreams.

This same scenario happens during the life cycle of a fetus developing in the mother's womb. During the developmental cycle, the fetus finds itself in a peaceful, comfortable, and safe environment, which encourages peaceful, comfortable, and safe dreams. It is not until the fetus leaves its mother's womb and is introduced to the world that its dreams and imagination are negatively affected, tampered with, or in some cases, destroyed. This is the moment where Satan begins to strategically plot, scheme, and use the sins of this world to destroy the imagination of men and women early in their lives. When we were in our mother's womb we were in a place where our thoughts were less likely to be negatively impacted.

Many adults today lack imagination because during their childhood, teenage, and young adult years, they kept their imagination and their hearts (or shall we say their minds) unprotected. This limited the scope of their ability to imagine. That's why it is important that we as children of God protect the precious God-given gift of imagination.

How do we protect our imagination? We protect it the same way that parents protect their beloved child. Your imagination is like your baby, and just like a baby, its development will depend on how well you nurture, protect, and feed it. You will either be a proud parent or a parent that mourns. *"Guard your heart above all else, for it determines your course of life"* (Prov. 4:23, NLT). Remember, our imagination lies within our heart, and the heart of man is our mind.

Think about this: Let's say that you input important data into a computer. A few weeks later you go to print the reports, but the data on the reports were incorrect. Do you get upset and kick the computer? Do you throw the computer into a burning fireplace? Do you talk badly about the computer and discredit the manufacturer? Why of course not.

Remember, you input the data, so if you received the wrong data output, that simply means that you incorrectly input the data. Many people have limited or negative imaginations because they have input negative things, circumstances, situations, and thoughts in their minds. Those same things are output. There was a saying I heard often growing up. Preachers, teachers, and many adults used to tell my friends and I to "guard our gates." Guard our gates? It actually sounded ridiculous without knowing the context in which it was being said. But in knowing the context the saying made sense.

We were told to guard our ear gates and eye gates for a reason. I soon learned that they were telling us to protect our eyes and ears from what we see and hear. Protecting your ear gates meant to limit what you heard to good things and protecting your eye gates meant to limit what you watched to good things. Our eyes and ears are the gateway to the mind, soul, and imagination. We have to be mindful of this and remember that Satan does not want us to use our imagination in the way that God intended. He uses our environment, media, some forms of music, family, friends, and other sources to put negative thoughts in our minds. Eventually these negative sources will destroy our imagination. This is why it is important that we surround ourselves with positive things and people.

Over the years, I've experienced the disappointments of having negative people in my life. Life-changing opportunities passed me by. Doors closed when I allowed others to negatively influence my imagination. Some people purposely did this while others did it unknowingly. Here's a story of how Satan's tactics almost destroyed my dreams.

When I was 10 years old, I imagined myself one-day having a successful music career as a recording artist, songwriter, and producer. So, I started writing songs, singing, and went to college and majored in Telecommunications and Music Engineering. Later, I landed an internship with a production duo team in Nashville, Tennessee. These producers poured so much knowledge and wisdom in to me about life as a musician and the music industry that I felt well equipped to begin my music career. They gave me opportunities to work with great Grammy winning recording artists. They helped me build relationships with many individuals in the industry and my musical resume. I was living my dream right out of college.

The years with those producers were some of the best years of my life. They even gave me my very own set of keys to their multi-million dollar studio and allowed me to come and go as I pleased. Unfortunately, sometime later I began to watch my dreams slip through my fingers because I was allowing the negative attitudes and mindsets of friends to manipulate me. I began feeling guilty about having the opportunities that they desired and it caused me to lose focus of the opportunities God had given ME. I was so concerned with helping friends get to a place that I hadn't yet reached; that my God-given opportunities were slipping away and my imagination, dreams and hope settled into a state of incapacitation.

This is a mistake that many of us make. Our emotions have a strange way of forcing our dreams and imaginations to the background while everything we're working for falls apart. We often see successful people on television bragging about bringing their friends along with them as they rise to success. However, we don't hear about the relationships that were destroyed and the numerous careers that crumbled along the way.

You have to remember that what God has for you, is for you and not for anyone else. Too often, our dreams are delayed or held hostage because of people that we are connected to who God has told and shown us we need to let go. It doesn't mean that these individuals are bad people; it may just mean that they are not a part of God's plan for us. However, be aware of Satan because he will try to make you feel as if you are not going to make it without them. Some of the hardest decisions that I've had to make in life were disconnecting from friends and loved ones who I cared deeply about, but were prohibited by God to go where he wanted to take me.

I recall one individual, who was one of the most talented music producers that I've ever met and an amazing friend to me. We had a great friendship and enjoyed fun times together. Whenever we were in the studio we created some of the most amazing recordings that still amaze me to this day. Our sound quality, creativity, and work ethic were so unique and respected that our clientele base grew rapidly.

As time went by, I began to hear a still quiet voice in my spirit tell me to release myself from the producer. Each time I heard this voice, I would ignore it simply because I refused to believe what I was hearing. How could I just leave a friend who had done nothing to me? If I did, what kind of friend would that make me? I prayed and cried and cried and prayed for answers. Why would God require this of me? As I continued to fight this request, our clientele base began to decrease. Clients stopped showing up and calling. I was baffled at how fast things went downhill and I did not understand why.

As time passed, it seemed as if every other day someone was pulling me to the side and telling me, "You need to release your friend." Mentors, friends, family, and God echoed this statement so loudly in my ear that I felt I was being haunted. But being a loyal friend, I ignored their advice.

It wasn't long until a woman with the gift of prophecy asked me a question that I will never forget.

This God-fearing woman came to my home, looked me in the eyes and asked, "TJ, why would you miss your Tuesday flight to where God has promised to take you, to take your friend to the bus station on Wednesday? When she said this, my knees began to buckle and tears formed in my eyes. I knew that very next day I had to release myself from that relationship. It hurt me to make that decision. I know it hurt him as well. I cried out to the Lord to help me understand why he required this of me. It was at that moment that I surrendered my life completely to God for ministry.

The decision to release myself from the working relationship put a serious strain on our friendship. However, a year later when I ran into those same artists who previously wouldn't return our phone calls, they explained why they never worked with us again. Every single client apologized for disappearing and not calling, but all admitted that it was something about my friend's spirit that made them uncomfortable. And because I was working with him, they no longer could work with me.

I admit I wanted to get upset for two reasons. One

reason was that I felt they could have just told me how they were feeling back then, instead of just detaching themselves. Secondly, they didn't know anything about my friend to justify judging him. However, I also knew that God gave me the same warnings, but I chose to ignore His voice and fight his request.

When I had finally had enough of dealing with the consequences of my disobedience, I made the very tough decision of asking him to move out. Almost immediately, God began to work extraordinary miracles in my life and to this day He continues to do so. I now realize that what God has for me is only for me—no one else.

Sometimes others are not meant to go with you. I tried so hard to be a loyal friend that I even tried pulling him into opportunities that God prepared for only me. I attempted to pull my friend in on projects, much to the objections of other producers. Eventually I stopped going to the studio regularly, because I didn't want to make my friend feel like I left him out. When the producers asked me to return the studio keys due to my inconsistency, I was stunned. I remember to this day, the moment I handed them over. Sometimes I think about where I would be today if I had not allowed my emotions and loyalty to others to get in the way of what God prepared for me.

It is also important to be careful of what we watch on television and cautious about the type of music to which we listen. If we don't guard our gates, Satan and his demonic angels along with their deceitful and manipulative ways, will seep into our gates and begin to strategically steal, kill, and destroy those very components of our mind that enhance our imagination. It is imperative that we stay mindful of this, because Satan knows that if he gets inside our thoughts, he can destroy our imagination. He makes us believe that what we imagine will never happen, or that it's foolish thinking, that it's not for persons like us, or that we don't deserve it. He will do whatever he can to make us doubt not only God, but ourselves as well!

Our environment is another tool that Satan uses. There are millions of people, young and old, whose environment has incapacitated their imagination, dreams and even their hope. They see negativity in their homes, neighborhoods, workplaces, and even in their own churches. If negativity is all that a person sees, then this is all the person will know. It is almost impossible to imagine anything better for yourself if you haven't seen something better.

The following chapters reveal ways to strengthen your imagination so that freely using it will become part of your lifestyle. By the end of this book, I hope your imagination is positive and real enough for you to believe that what you imagine can become reality.

3

Strengthened

> "Imagination is like a muscle. I found out that the more I wrote the bigger it got."
> —Phillip José Farmer

There is a reason why you are reading this book. It may be different from someone else who is also reading it. You recognize the importance of your imagination. You also understand that if you don't strengthen your imagination, you have little to strive for.

It's amazing how we desire great things, but we neglect to take the necessary steps to get them. You must first strengthen your imagination. To strengthen anything, there has to be a willingness to do it, partnered with effort, patience and perseverance. Strengthening takes strength; you have to be mentally strong. You need to know what you want and what it takes to get it, and you have to use both to make it happen.

In this chapter, I want to teach you how to strengthen your imagination. I will introduce techniques that will help you enhance it. Again, you have to be willing. Some of the things that I will suggest may sound silly and even stupid. You might think it's just a waste of your time. However, these techniques, if used properly, will open up a whole new world and way of thinking for you. Are you ready? Let's explore.

1. Acknowledge the Power of Imagination

The first and most important step in strengthening your imagination is to acknowledge its power. You have to believe that your imagination is more than a thought, and much more than a dream. Your imagination is waiting to become reality. That's right, *reality*. Your dreams can become reality through your imagination. While, some of the things you imagine may seem far-fetched, there is nothing too far-fetched for God. Remember, *"We can do all things through Christ who strengthens us" (Phil. 4:13)*.

In the late 1800's to early 1900's there were two brothers who had extraordinary imaginations. During their youth, these brothers were always fascinated with mechanics, taking things apart, and putting them back together. Even though these two young men never received high school diplomas, they did not stop gaining knowledge and using it to become very successful in all of their endeavors. In 1892, the brothers opened a bicycle repair and sales shop called, "The Wright Cycle Exchange." They later changed the name to "The Wright Cycle Company" and started manufacturing bicycles.

Before establishing the bicycle shop, the brothers also started a very successful newspaper print shop, "West Side News." You can already see the benefits and progression of their imaginations.

In 1878, their father, who traveled often due to ministry, came home from a long trip and brought the brothers a toy helicopter. When the helicopter broke, they built their own. In later years, their experience with the toy helicopter sparked an interest in flying. If you have not figured it out, or do not know, I'm making reference to the famous *Wright Brothers.* They are known for and credited with inventing the airplane. Many say they invented the first flying aircraft, but the truth is that they did not.

In the mid 1890's a man named Otto Lilienthal from Germany invented the first "gliding flight" apparatus. The gliding flight was an unpowered aircraft that was the precursor to the hand-gliders, hot air balloons, and even parachutes. Many people were killed while flying these gliders, including the inventor Lilienthal. The Wright Brothers set out to find an improved way to control the inflight aircraft.

One day Wilbur Wright saw birds flying in the sky. He closely observed how the birds used their wings to turn to the left and right, and how they used them to fly upwards, and downwards. He also observed how they used their wings to land. The brothers then concluded that if they used the same concepts for an aircraft, the aircraft would be easier and safer to control. Today, we have airplanes and enjoy the luxury of flying to various destinations around the world in record time. It all came to fruition through what the Wright brothers imagined spoke and put into action. Which brings us to the second step for strengthening your imagination— the "what if."

2. The "What If"

Let's again use the Wright brothers as an example.

As stated earlier, these brothers were introduced to a flying aircraft called the *glider*. The device intrigued them, however it had numerous flaws. This is where their imagination kicked in. They imagined, what if the aircraft had wings like a bird, and what if the one flying the aircraft could control it like a bird controls its wings. This is why airplanes have wings. The Wright brothers created the airplane not by chance, but by asking the question, "What if?" This question is where imagination begins to generate creativity.

It's the "what if" question that triggers your imagination to flow with images and ideas that have not yet been created. Many of the inventions we've used for centuries (and will continue to use for years to come) were *imagined* by people who asked the question, "What if?" The Wright brothers did nothing more than stretch their imagination further than the previous inventor of the glider. You too can find something that has already been created, and ask yourself, "What if I made improvements to an object such as a car or something else? What would those improvements be?" You get the point.

Now try this. Write down the names of three ideas

in the following spaces. Under each listed idea, write a "What if" question. Then answer the "What if" question. For example, let's say that you wrote the word "car" as your idea, and your "what if" question for that car is, "What if this car had wings?" Answer the question with all of the possibilities for how a car with wings could benefit the driver. Repeat this process for all three ideas. It doesn't matter how crazy the "What if?" questions sound; write them down anyway.

Idea #1 _____

_____

What if _____

_____

Answer _____

_____

Idea #2 _____

_____

What if _____

_____

Answer _____

_____

Idea #3 _____

_____

What if _____

_____

Answer _____

_____

This exercise will help stretch your imagination and lead you to think outside the box. Who knows, something you imagine could possibly change the course of your life or be the next multi billion-dollar invention. To be honest, the more out of the box your ideas are, the better. You want to stretch your imagination as far as you can—the further the better and the more exciting. Enjoy this experience. Your imagination will help you see things, your life and the world differently. The imagination is so powerful that if used properly, it can mentally take you to another place, far away from your current position, circumstances, and life issues. That's right; your imagination can rescue you at least for a moment from the hurt, pain, and trouble that reality can bring. If you need to just get away from it all and gain peace of mind, your imagination can help you do so.

Again, the first step to strengthening the imagination is to believe in it and acknowledge the power that it holds. The second step is to ask the question, "What if?" The third step involves the use of "the arts."

3. The Arts

The arts can drive our imaginations in ways that nothing else can. There are many components to the arts, such as: theater, music, painting, and drawing. I believe music is one of the most influential art forms of our imagination. Music can spark ideas and emotions. Yes, MUSIC! Music is the art of sound in time that expresses ideas and emotions in significant forms through the elements of rhythm, melody, harmony, and color (www.dictionary.com).

Music has a way of fueling our imagination, and emotions in ways that are unexplainable. It can make you feel a variety of emotions. Research shows that listening to classical music can stimulate the right side of your brain, which supports the thought process.

Have you ever heard a song on the radio, or played a CD, or maybe heard a song on television and immediately images came to your mind? Maybe it was a Christmas song that took you back to a childhood moment when you were opening gifts under the Christmas tree with your family; or maybe it was a love song that reminded you of your first crush, date, or kiss. Perhaps it was a hymn that reminded you of your dear grandmother or grandfather. In any case, that song or melody was linked to a memory that helped you relive a moment that made you smile or even cry. That is an example of how music can connect with your imagination.

Using music, the next exercise will take imagination to another level. I've used this exercise to comfort and calm myself when things were not going well. I hope and pray that you will experience similar results. Your imagination will be pushed farther, so try to step out of your comfort zone.

Instructions

Preferably, choose instrumental music (without lyrics) so that your mind is not influenced by what the lyricist imagined when writing the lyrics. Allow the rhythm, melody, harmony, and color of the song to inspire your ideas and emotions. To avoid interruptions, try this when home alone, turn off your cell phone, unplug the landline phone, and turn off the television. If you have a good pair of headphones, put them on as well, then lay back and relax. If you do not have headphones, just turn the music on.

Now, allow your imagination to take over. Try this for 30-minutes to an hour then turn off the music. While sitting quietly with no interruptions, respond to the following questions:

Question # 1: How do you feel?

Question # 2: What did you see?

Question # 3: Where were you?
(Imaginary Place)

Question #4: Who was there?

Step out of your normal thinking mode to get the most out of this exercise. This is important because you have to separate reality from imagination. For example, if you have an urban lifestyle, live in an urban community, and listen to urban music, you may want to imagine yourself being a wealthy conservative, with few worries, living in a mansion with the finest furnishings, who enjoys less contemporary music.

Or, you may have a conservative lifestyle. If that's the case, you may want to imagine being a laid back liberal who values life and family most, enjoys listening to jazz and sitting on his or her back porch near the pool, while food is cooking on the grill. Whatever and however you decide you want to feel, the type of person you want to be, and where you want to be, make sure to select the type of music that fits that personality and situation. Keep a dated record of it and note the time on it. Keep this in a journal or diary and do this exercise often. By doing so, you are writing down your vision and making it plain (Habakkuk 2:2). Everyday life has a way of making us forget those things that make us happy. Documenting what you imagined will give you the opportunity to go back and relive that moment in the future.

Remember these exercises and practice them often. They will not only help you find peace of mind, but they will also strengthen your imagination. Using it will become second nature. The "What if?" exercise will not only help you discover other options and new opportunities, but will also help you in *problem solving*, which will be covered within the next few chapters.

When life brings you lemons, make lemonade. When life deals you a bad hand, you play that hand the best you can. Life is unpredictable, and we never know what it will bring. Again, Satan wants to steal, kill, and destroy not only our imagination, but also our lives. He does not want us to have from life what God desires for us. He gets into our minds and wreaks havoc. He tries to discourage us, make us doubt God, loved ones, and ourselves. "The thief cometh not, but for to steal, and to kill, and to destroy: I am come that they might have life, and that they might have it more abundantly" (John 10:10, KJV).

Even though Satan's plan is to destroy us, God said that he comes to give us life. Not just any life, but life more abundantly! *Abundant* means present in great quantity, more than adequate; overflowing, more than sufficient, abounding, richly supplied. It means to have more then we could ever imagine. *No eye has seen, no ear has heard, no mind has conceived what God has prepared for those who love Him" (1 Cor. 2:9, NIV).* We may never be able to conceive all the wonderful things that God has for us, but nothing can stop us from imagining what those things could possibly be. That's the greatest thing about imagination. There is no limit!

4

Inhibited By Hoarding

> **"Live out your imagination, not your history."**
> **–Stephen Covey**

It was 3:00 am in the morning when I opened my watery eyes. I had no idea that I was crying in my sleep. I awoke in my hospital bed, two weeks had passed and I was still in recovery. Oh how badly I wanted to be home, in my own bed, and with my family. I began to think about all of the young people my father had buried with the same gunshot womb that I had, but for some reason I was still alive. I thought about how many of those gunshot victims that he had buried died due to their participation in violence. But there I was, a victim despite not being involved in the violence. Though I was in pain, I slowly reached over and picked up the receiver to the telephone that was on the side table next to my bed, and I dialed my home number. Nervously, I waited for someone to pick up the phone because

I knew that it was early in the morning, but I had to talk to someone. Suddenly, someone with a very groggy voice answered the phone and said, "hello?" It was my father. Oh my, I was so happy to hear his voice. I felt so alone in that dark room all by myself. When I responded with a hello, he immediately asked, "what's wrong?" The first words that came out of my mouth was, "why me?" There was a moment of silence as if he was stunned by the question. Tears continued to stream down my face as I waited for the answer. To my surprise his answer was far from what I expected. I was expecting a deep answer, a profound revelation, a confident explanation, but all I heard was reluctance in his voice when he responded with, "I don't know?" You don't know? How could he not know, I mean didn't he have a direct line to God? I mean, come on, not only was he my father, but my pastor. How could he not know? My father knew everything! He had always had the answer or the solution to any problem; but here I was, laying on what could have potentially been my deathbed at the most critical time in my life and the only thing he had to give me was a pain filled response of, "I don't know." Talk about a blow to the gut! Not only did this answer frustrate me, but it hurt me as well. Though his answer was disappointing, he did continue on to say, "T.J., I can't tell you why this has happened to you, but I can tell you that if you continue to live, pray and serve God, one day He will reveal to you the answer to your question. That still wasn't the answer I wanted; however it did make sense. Knowing why God does some things and allows certain things to happen is none of our business. Our responsibility is to trust Him and lean not to our own understanding, but trust him and He will direct our path in life (Proverbs 3:5-6). I realize now that Satan was trying to cast doubt in my mind and spirit, and if I would have allowed those negative thoughts to fester, it could have possibly hindered not only my recovery but my future.

Life is unpredictable. We experience ups and downs. We have good days, and we have bad ones, but I am so glad that the word of God reminds us that, *"All things work together for the good of those who love God, to them who are the called according to His purpose" (Romans 8:28, KJV).* Yes, all things that include the bad, the ugly, the disappointments and the things that break our hearts and often discourage us.

It doesn't matter how bad things are, they all work together for our benefit, if we love God with all of our heart, mind, and soul.

I've learned a lot in my lifetime, but one of the most important things I've learned is that we can't always control what happens to us; we can only control how we deal with what happens to us. How we handle the circumstances in our lives will determine how they are resolved, and how they are resolved depends on whose word you will trust. Will you trust the God who knows your beginning and your end or will you trust Satan whose main purpose is to destroy you? The choice is yours.

Job 14:1 says, *"Man that is born of a woman is of a few days, and full of trouble" (KJV).* Job is basically saying that all of us are on this earth for a specific amount of time, and during this time span we are surrounded by trouble. So, the question is, when we run into these troubles, issues, and circumstances, how will we allow them to affect us? Our time on earth is short, and we can allow the troubles of life to have either a positive or negative effect on our lives and imaginations.

In the last few months, I have viewed television shows, movies, talk and intervention shows that focused on the issue of *hoarding*. Hoarding has become a big topic in the media. Many "hoarders" have lost their families, jobs, homes, valuable possessions, and even their minds because of this horrific problem. The media has drawn considerable attention to the issue and we are hearing about it more often, but the truth of the matter is that hoarders have been around for years, decades, and even centuries.

A hoarder is someone who accumulates things, hides items, collects anything, which he or she considers valuable, and then stores it for future use. The problem is that a majority of hoarders never use the "valuables" they have stored away. Hoarders viewed on television accumulate so much stuff that it becomes embarrassing, unhealthy, and sometimes downright disgusting. Many of their homes have every room literally filled from the floor to the ceiling with old clothes, food, toys, garbage, books, used diapers and anything else imaginable. Many of these people once thought that their cat or dog had run away from home, only to find the skeletal remains of their dead pet underneath the junk and garbage that they had accumulated.

You are probably wondering how someone could allow his or her life to get to this state. Well, after watching a number of television shows and reading up on the issue, I think I've discovered an answer to the question.

Every hoarder has a different reason for why they hoard. Life experiences have influenced many. There was the story of a woman who was such a hoarder that her landlord sued her. She had so much stuff piled up in her house that there was a foul odor seeping out of the house and into the neighborhood. Rodents and roaches were plentiful and because of negligence, the house was severely damaged. Not only did the landlord sue this woman, but a storage company also sued her. Since she had no more room left in her home for storage, she rented storage units and the same hoarding scenario occurred in the facility. She had seven refrigerators that were so full of spoiled and rotten food that she resorted to keeping food in her car in the wintertime to keep it cold. I know this is shocking and hard to believe, but it is reality, and it is how many people today are living. Many hoarders will give up on themselves and let their family go, before they give up or let go of any of their many possessions. They value their possessions more than the people in their lives.

You may be wondering what all of this has to do with imagination. Believe it or not, the idea of hoarding has a lot to do with imagination. Now that you have an idea of what hoarding is, and what behaviors determine that an individual is a hoarder, you can better understand how that same behavior can affect our imagination.

A key point about hoarding is that the behavior does not start overnight. Habits are developed over a period of time. People develop habits for various reasons. I have described the lifestyle of a hoarder, but let's go a little deeper and see what causes people to become hoarders.

Here are a few possible examples of why a person becomes a hoarder. A potential hoarder grew up in a family that didn't have much. They were classified as poor. No matter how hard the parents worked, they never seemed to have enough money to make ends meet. It was a rough childhood and he or she was told they would never grow up to amount to anything or that he or she would always be poor.

Fortunately, for some, that was not true. Somehow, they were able to overcome the negativity and achieve success. Through their success came money they used to purchase the things that they desired but were not able to have when they were poor. Perhaps, this is one reason why many hoarders hold on to everything. They never had anything nice while growing up and what they owned was limited, so they don't want to get rid of what they have now. They want to hold onto things for fear of losing them, and since they don't want to give anything away, it accumulates and piles up in their homes.

Over a course of years, their homes will look like the woman's home I described earlier. Speaking of that woman, her process of becoming a hoarder was a little different. The woman grew up and had it made. She was raised in a wealthy and loving family, attended the best private schools, lived in the best homes, and never had to want for anything. However, over her lifetime, her family lost their wealth, her mother and father became sick, and soon died. Her siblings and other family members also died. She had a great career but lost it too. She had wonderful friendships that became distant, and soon she found herself alone.

This lady had lost so much in her life that she was determined to never lose anything else, so she began to acquire and store possessions. She also stored items that belonged to love ones who had passed away, because she felt closer to them by hoarding their possessions, even if she couldn't find or enjoy them among the clutter. These items held memories that she was afraid she might lose if she got rid of them. It is easy to judge people and their issues, but we never know the underlying reasons of why they are the way they are, or how they ended up in these unfortunate situations.

You may still be asking what this has to do with imagination. Well, for many of us our imaginations are limited because of our past life experiences. Many people have had bad childhood experiences, have lived in poverty or perhaps have been a victim of rape, molestation, or abuse. Situations, such as these, have negatively affected their mindset and self-esteem, and in turn their imagination. They have no vision, no dreams and no hope. Perhaps there is a young man who grew up in a home where his father was a drunk, in and out of prison; or his mother was a streetwalker and drug addict. All that he heard while growing up was that he was going to be just like his "no good" parents. He heard this from family members, his teachers, and friends. Because he heard this all of his life, he began to believe it in his heart (mind) and it was all that he could imagine for himself. He couldn't imagine anything beyond what had been instilled in his heart regarding his future.

Maybe these examples do not fit your life, and you can't relate, but perhaps there is something that has happened in your life that has affected you mentally, emotionally, physically or spiritually. Maybe you have accumulated all those years of negative thoughts and memories, and it is hard for you to imagine anything better for yourself. Have you collected those negative words spoken to you and negative things done to you over the years? Have you allowed those memories to accumulate in your mind? If this is you, then guess what? You are a hoarder. That's right, a hoarder. Remember, a hoarder is someone who accumulates, hides, and collects.

What memories are you hoarding? What emotions are you hiding behind your smile? Look very hard and deep within your soul and check to see if you have become a hoarder of negative experiences that have accumulated over time. Those experiences have affected your way of thinking and your way of living. If this is you, then my prayer is that by the end of this book, you will have released and let go of those things. It is also my prayer that you will have cleaned out the negative thoughts and emotions and beliefs that have accumulated in your memory bank. You are created for greatness and you are purposefully and specially made. The sky is the limit for you. Negative thinking and damaged emotions will not benefit your imagination and the things that it can add to your life. Remember, faith and imagination go hand and hand. We must hope for what we imagine until it becomes evident in our lives.

Lastly, we have to forgive those who have hurt us. God cannot and will not work through someone with an unforgiving heart. There are so many miracles that are hindered simply because people will not forgive. The Lord is big on forgiveness. Just think of all the times he has forgiven us. In Matthew 18, Peter asked Jesus how many times he should forgive his brother or sister who sins against him. Jesus' reply was to forgive them seventy-seven times.

Jesus is extremely serious when it comes to forgiveness. He is so serious that when He was crucified on the cross for our sins and charged with a crime he did not commit, He chose to forgive instead of getting angry with those who persecuted him. He looked up to heaven and asked our heavenly Father to forgive them because they didn't know nor understood the mistake that they were making (Luke 23:34). That's true forgiveness. How many of us could have done that? Could you? I know how extremely difficult it would be to utter those words while being murdered for something I didn't do. However, Jesus did it because He wanted us to be saved and have eternal life.

Sometimes we live with the hurt so long that it becomes apart of who we are and we began to think that the pain is normal. Besides, if we let it go and forgive, who will we be able to blame for our failures and our unfulfilled potential? Sometimes we hold on to the hurt so long that we don't realize that the hurt is being disguised as anger. We lash out at others for no reason, we take offense when others are trying to help us and we make it a point to discredit others just because we are hurting. There is a saying that says, "Hurt people, hurt people," and I have found much truth in those words.

Ask yourself this question: Are your goals and dreams so important to you that you are willing to forgive those who have sinned against you? If your answer is "No," then go to God and ask Him to help you forgive them. Please, forgive them! Before you go on to the next chapter, release the pain, disappointment, and anger you may be holding on to. Give it to God. If you don't, you may be hindering what God can and wants to do through your imagination and your life. Letting go and forgiveness is not only a gift to the other person, but it's also a gift to you.

5

Purpose-Given

> "Imagination will often carry us to worlds that never were. But without it we go nowhere."
> -Carl Sagan

God does everything for a purpose. Although we may never know why He does the things He does, we should rest assured that there is a reason behind it. From the beginning of this book we have discussed much about imagination, from its importance to ways to protect it. However, if we don't know the purpose of that which we are strengthening and protecting, we may not know the value of what we have. Knowing the value of our imagination will make strengthening and protecting it more of a necessity.

When we talk about the word *"purpose"* we are talking about the reason why something exists, is made, or is completed. We are also talking about something that was intended. When God gave us imagination, he intended for us to do something with it. The purpose for it within each person might be different in detail, but is the same when it comes to benefiting the Kingdom of God. Our purpose on this earth is to worship God and serve others. We worship God through obedience and we use our imagination to make the worship experience that much greater.

There have been times during worship that my imagination has taken over and pushed me through a threshold that seemed to have kept me from reaching my breakthrough. Using my imagination somehow blocked out the world around me, and escorted me to the spiritual realm of deliverance that I needed. When I worshiped while in the need of deliverance, I raised my hands in praise and imagined God's hand reaching down to pull me up. When I worshiped in loneliness and opened my arms in worship, I imagined the Lord accepting my invitation to come close, hug and hold me. This may sound ridiculous to some, but this is how my imagination has enhanced my worship.

I have read and heard about the wonders of heaven

and the beauty that it beholds. I've literally pictured myself walking the streets of transparent gold, admiring the gates and walls full of precious stones and clear crystal waters, and living in a place where death and weeping do not exist. I've imagined myself there in order to motivate myself to do whatever necessary to make sure that heaven becomes my future home.

Understand and remember that heaven should be our goal. This earth is not our home. This is just a pit stop on our journey to the place that God has prepared for us. In order to reach that place, we must be obedient, have faith, and use our imagination to help build faith. God the Father is in that place, and we know that in order to see Him, we must go through Jesus who says, *"I am the truth and the life. No one comes to the Father except through me" (John 14:6).*

There are things that Jesus requires of us to get through Him, and it's as simple as A,B,C. (A) ACCEPT Jesus as your Lord and personal Savior, (B) BELIEVE in your heart that He died and was resurrected for your sins, and (C) CONFESS it with your mouth, in other words share your salvation and belief with others. We have to study the Word and use our imagination to apply it to our lives to reach heaven.

Scripture repeatedly encourages us to serve others. Jesus gave the greatest command when He admonished us to love the Lord with all our heart, soul and mind (Matt. 22:36-40). This Scripture appears to sum up the purpose not only for our lifestyle, but also for our imagination and the use of it.

We've already talked about using imagination for worshiping and loving God. It should also be used to serve sisters and brothers in Christ. We can worship and love God all day long, however, we are also called to love our brothers and sisters (1 John 4:20). What better way to show love for others than by serving them?

Jesus was a servant to all with whom He came in contact with. When people needed healing, He healed them; when they needed guidance, He guided them; when they needed a blessing, He blessed them. He gave food to the hungry and sight to the blind.. He served everyone, even those who did not believe in Him.

There is nothing wrong with using imagination for personal gain; however, from that gain we should serve others. There are millions of people whose imaginations have helped them gain great wealth, but they have used that wealth to benefit only themselves. If imagination is God-given, it should be used in the same way that God uses it. Everything God created through divine imagination was done so for us to enjoy and to meet our needs.

After God created Adam and Eve in his own image He told them to be fruitful and multiply, replenish the earth, subdue it; have dominion over the fish of the sea, the fowl of the air, and over every living thing that moves on earth (Gen. 1:28). God imagined and created everything to serve us and meet our needs. He expects us to do the same by serving and meeting the needs of others.

So how do we use imagination to serve others? Well, before we start trying to save people's lives and serve them, we need to go back to the basics of study and meditation on God's Word. Here's an interesting note: I found an acronym for "BIBLE" that stands for "**B**asic **I**nstructions **B**efore **L**eaving **E**arth." That makes sense. If you believe the Bible then you know that everyone has to leave this earth one day; and after death comes judgment. Whether your soul ends up in heaven or hell is determined by your acceptance of Jesus Christ as Lord and Savior, and how you lived your life on earth.

Of course, God's desire is to have all of His children in heaven with Him, but we also know that at the end of it all, everyone will not make it to heaven. We have to use God's Word as the basis of serving and allow imagination to help us be creative in how we actually serve. I love how the apostle Paul became weak to win the weak, and became all things to all men by all means possible to save some (1 Cor. 9:22). This is an example of Paul using his imagination to help save diverse people with varying lifestyles and circumstances.

Paul was not saying that he would dismiss his morality and beliefs in order to conform to the sinful lifestyle of an individual. Instead, he was referring to positioning himself to be able to relate to people regardless of their existing condition. He met them where they were. To do what Paul said he did, defi-

nitely required use of imagination. If he was trying
to win the weak to salvation, we know he had to be
strong spiritually, yet weak to relate to them.

Of course this sounds like an oxymoron, but I believe this is where Paul had to use imagination. He
had to imagine himself in a place where he was once
weak, wanting to give up, or during a time when he
needed God to take away a thorn in his life in order for him to relate to a person who felt the same.
Perhaps Paul had to tap into weak moments and
emotions in his life in order to empathize with the
weak because he too had been there. He could then
explain to them how he came out of it by relying on
God's Word and promises. I don't know how Paul
used his imagination, but I am confident that he
used it to serve and relate to people in need.

We will encounter many people who will want to
give up on life, walk away from their families, commit unlawful acts, along with other things. By using
imagination, we can help them find new opportunities and possibilities. We can help them get through
their circumstances by pointing to Jesus as their es-
cape. The greatest service we can do for the unsaved

is to lead them to salvation. The greatest service we can do for those already saved is to encourage them to continue in faithful obedience.

Finally, I believe that another purpose for imagination is to lead us to renewed understanding of and revelation from the Scriptures. Have you ever read a Scripture and received a revelation from it, then later read the same Scripture and received a totally different revelation? This is an example of how God will use imagination to bring new revelation to us when we seek His knowledge through Scripture. The more we use it as we read God's Word, the more we will find ourselves getting excited about His promises for our lives. The more excited we get, the more we will desire to live to please Him. Hebrews 11:6 tells us that "without faith it is impossible to please God..." If we want God to be pleased with us, we have to exercise faith. Imagination and life experiences strengthen our faith.

There are some things that we desire for our lives, and we have faith that it will happen, but when it finally happens we aren't ready for it. This is another reason why imagination is important. Imagination will keep us excited and focused on what we believe will happen. And when it does come into fruition, our imagination has already created a plan of action.

I want to share a very special testimony that reinforces how the power and purpose of imagination worked an amazing miracle in my life.

On June 5, 2010, before hundreds of friends and family members I married my girlfriend of four years. It was a moment that I will never forget. After four years of ups and downs, fasting and praying, God finally gave me His grace to ask Demetria Ruffin, now Demetria Jordan, to be my wife. There were times during our dating period when we didn't know if we would make it as a couple, but deep down inside we just knew that we were destined to be together. While dating, we often talked about what we thought marriage would be like. I still laugh when I think of some of the things we came up with!

Even when we disagreed on certain things, there was one thing that we were certain of, and that was having children. Before marriage we had already chosen names for our future children and were waiting for that moment to tattoo those names to their very existence. Two years into our marriage we decided we were ready for children.

To make a long story short, we were reminded by doctors of the various medical challenges that my wife had endured and feared that these issues would hinder us from ever having children. We tried over and over again, but it just seemed as if we would never experience the blessing of parenthood. It was at this point that my faith and imagination began to kick in. I thought of how we had imagined and spoken children into our life during our entire courtship. While dating we practiced celibacy, prayed together, fasted, and stayed faithful to God. Yes, we were discouraged every now and then, but we kept on believing and trusting God.

During our time of trying, I lost my grandfather and he was laid to rest on May 5, 2012. This was a very difficult time for my family and I, but we celebrated his life and legacy with true praise and worship. Eight days later, Sunday, May 13, 2012, my wife and I celebrated Mother's Day with our mothers, surprising them with a variety of special gifts. Little did my wife know that she too was expecting a surprise gift.

I woke early Mother's Day morning, and while my wife was getting ready for church I handed her a card. She opened the colorful card that said "Happy Mother's Day", looked at the bottom of it and saw the names of our children written in child-like form, as if they had signed their names themselves. She began to cry. Immediately, I thought to myself, "Oh, I think I just made a mistake. I think I may have just offended her!" Suddenly, she looked at me with tears in her eyes and said, "This is the most beautiful thing that I have ever received." Whew! You should have seen the look of relief on my face. Then she said, "But TJ, I am not a mother." I looked at her and said, "Yes you are!" And when she gave me a kiss and a hug, I felt like the luckiest husband in the world.

On June 19, 2012, at 5:39 p.m. I was at work getting ready for a presentation. My phone rang and at the other end of the phone was my wife's sweet voice. When I greeted her she said to me, "Hey babe, Listen, I am going to text you something, but please don't show anyone the text." I hung up the phone and a few seconds later I opened the text that she sent. The text was a picture of a pregnancy test she took indicating that she was pregnant!

At that moment any man that had experienced the extended waiting period we had would have probably run around the room like an excited crazed man, but I did not. Immediately, I said, "Thank you Jesus", then responded to my wife's text with a simple, "I told you so!" We kept this secret until we received confirmation two weeks later from her doctor. Praise God! We were so happy and thankful. We prayed and thanked the Lord for keeping His promise to us.

Shortly after receiving the news, we were hit with something ironic. Curious to know when we actually conceived, my wife, a master with numbers, calculated the date of conception and found out that it was the same day that we buried my grandfather! Isn't that interesting? I had been told that usually when someone dies, new birth is right around the corner. This is another example of how imagining something, speaking it, and being obedient can bring things imagined into fruition. When it came to my wife and I having a child, I used my imagination like never before. My wife can tell you, I talked to our imaginary children, they rode in the car with me, I wrote a beautiful song for them, I prayed with them, and I played with them. I did this so much that I began to really believe that they actually existed.

When I gave my wife that mother's day card, she was a mother— carrying our unborn daughter. Our story co-signs the Scripture, "As it is written: "I have made you a father of many nations. He is our father in the sight of God, in whom he believed-the God who gives life to the dead and calls things that are not as though they were" (Romans 4:17).

Paul reminds us that Abraham trusted God and believed that He would deliver on His promise to him. I'm convinced that Abraham was reminded of how God imagined and spoke this world into existence, and he trusted that God could do the same in his life. And even though Abraham's physical state looked as though it contradicted what God had promised, Abraham's faith proved that God always keeps His word. These two stories demonstrate how imagination and faith have ushered realities into the lives of God's children.

I hope that you have received a revelation about your purpose given imagination. Remember that God wants us to use it for kingdom building, worshiping him and serving others.

6

Childlike In Nature

> "So like a forgotten fire, a childhood can always flare up again within us."
> -Gaston Bachelard

Have you ever closed your eyes and listened to children playing together? Did you hear the happiness in their laughter, the excitement of their playfulness, and feel the warmth in their smiles? I know there are times when we are around children who are playing and laughing, and suddenly we catch ourselves smiling and laughing, as well. At that moment we have just joined the spirit of their environment without even realizing it. There is something calming about the innocence of their lives and the fearlessness of their play. I don't know what it is that makes us melt when we see children at play, but we can almost become a little envious when we see their happiness and carefree existence. It's as if they have no cares in the world.

There was a time when we were in that place of carefree play and imagination without worry. The children of today will one day walk in our shoes and have to wrestle with the cares of this world. For now, let's rejoice and encourage them to have fun, dream big, and unleash their imaginations.

Do you remember those days when it seemed like time just flew by when you were playing and having fun? I do. I guess the saying "time flies when you're having fun" is true. Oh, how I wish I could relive the memories and moments I had when my imagination took hold of me! I can still remember many of the things that I imagined when I was a little boy, and to be honest, I am living the realization of some of those memories today. I know for sure that what we imagine can become true.

It is easy to allow the worries and cares of this world to kidnap and hold captive imagined things that helped us laugh and live freely. Where did it go and how do we get it back? That is a good question that we all need to ask ourselves. We need to do whatever it takes to get it back, because we need it. With all of the things that life throws our way—challenges, heartaches and disappointments—we need to access and draw from our imaginations.

Somewhere during the maturing process from childhood to adulthood, we seem to have lost the fuel that kept our imagination active. While we can't go back physically to our childhood, we can go back in our hearts and minds, which can be as good as becoming a child again. Oh, yes we can! There was the fuel that kept our imagination active and real when we were children. We had this "thing" even then but didn't know it. We didn't even know what it was and we certainly didn't know that in order to get through life with peace of mind, we would need it.

This "thing" that I am referring to is *faith*. Oh yes, faith. We have touched on it lightly in previous chapters, but faith can't be used lightly. Faith is the only thing that will strengthen and reintroduce us to that childhood imagination that made us believe the unbelievable and embrace the impossible. As children, we didn't know what faith was, but we used it.

"Faith is the substance of things hoped for…" (Heb. 11:1). Hope is the feeling that something can be. As children, we imagined having something and being someone special. We didn't consider that there was a chance that it wouldn't work out. We felt within ourselves that it would happen. It was the feeling that strengthened our faith. It was the feeling of excitement and comfort that made us believe. We need to get that feeling back and fight for it with everything that we have. We need to pray for it and ask God to give back every part of the feeling that the devil stole.

Feeling (emotions) is a sensation that does not come from any of our 5 senses. It doesn't come from a touch; it's something that comes from within, from that place only God created. It comes from our soul, and our desires. Many adults have lost this feeling and that is why we don't believe in what we imagine in the same way that we believed as children. Ask God for it, believing you will receive it back.

Someone may be reading this and quoting, *"When I was a child, I spoke as a child, I understood as a child, I thought as a child; but when I became a man, I put away childish things"* (1 Cor. 13:11). If this is you, then understand that the power of imagination has nothing to do with the immaturity of being a child; it's about having imagination *like* a child. God wants us all to have hearts like children. Matthew 18:4 says *"Therefore, whoever humbles himself like this child is the greatest in the kingdom of heaven."* God wants us to have a childlike heart and to use our imagination much like we did as children.

A child's faith is strong when they imagine they are invincible. I mentioned in the beginning of this book that I used to watch Kung Fu movies and that after every movie my confidence level was so high, I felt I could beat up anybody. There was something about those movies that influenced me to think that I could do it. Of course, I know now that if I had to fight someone bigger or someone actually trained in Kung Fu, I would not have stood a chance. However, you couldn't convince me otherwise at the time.

Just as I believed I was invincible as a child, we have to believe in what we imagine for our lives now. We have to be confident in what we believe and not allow others to deter us or cast doubt. I don't care what it is. If you see yourself getting out of debt, then you can; if you see God mending your broken home, then He can. If you see yourself starting your own business, then it is possible. All things are possible with God and faith. If you believe in something and you put hard work behind it, then what you imagine is alive. "Faith without works is dead" (Jas. 2:20). Let's go deep into our soul and find that inner child that we once knew. Allow that child to lead us back into a world of faith where the impossible was possible and what we imagined in our minds was real to us.

7

A Succession Plan

> **"You don't have to be dead to live a legacy."**
> **–Onyi Anyado**

One of the greatest accomplishments achieved in my lifetime was receiving a formal education. My parents instilled in me at an early age the importance of getting a good education and the benefits of having it. They made certain that I studied, did my homework, paid attention and respected my teachers, and brought home good grades. And while I was not an honor student, I was an average student who successfully graduated from high school and college.

Graduation was not an option for my siblings and I— it was a requirement! If we were going to eat our parent's food and sleep under their roof we had better graduate. I admit some high school and college courses highly challenged me, but I never gave up. I will always remember both graduations because

I worked hard to earn them and walked across both stages. No one can ever take those achievements away from me.

I am grateful that my parents and teachers poured into me. I would not be where I am today if they had not. My parents were examples of successful college graduates. As a more visual learner, I paid attention to their lifestyles—how they treated others, raised my siblings and I, their work ethic, and most importantly, their love for God.

Many years have passed since I graduated from college. Being older and wiser, I now know that success and a good life are not based on graduating from an educational institution. A formal education will help elevate a person in life, however, it is not the piece of paper you receive that gets you there; it is belief and determination. There are many people, who will totally disagree with me on this, but I know for a fact that there are numerous high school and college drop outs that are living enjoyable and even lucrative lifestyles simply because they used imagination, determination, and believed they would succeed. I graduated because I imagined and believed that I would and did the work.

Many parents invest in their children's education often spending enormous amounts of money to send their children to prestigious schools and universities around the world. These parents want their children to have the best, but do they ever stop to think or consider what it is that their child really wants? Some parents find out that they have spent thousands of dollars for a formal education that their child will never use. Let's be real, just because you received a degree doesn't mean that you really learned anything significant that will ensure success.

College exposed me to things that fueled my imagination and presented me with options. My hometown seemed to box in my imagination. From my view, it looked as if everyone acted the same way, lived the same way, and thought the same way. If my parents had not exposed my siblings and I to family vacations, music, movies, education, and diverse people, my imagination would probably still be boxed in. They were determined to expose us to opportunities the world held, and I'm determined to do the same for my children and grandchildren. It is vital that we leave a blueprint for future generations.

When you die, what legacy will you leave your children, grandchildren, or even strangers? Of course, you can prepare a will, leave them a house, money, and other material things, but those things can perish. It is similar to the old saying, "Give a man a fish and he will eat for a day. Teach him how to fish and he will eat for a lifetime." Within the same context, you can teach others how to continue using their imagination long after you die. Why not have a succession plan, teach someone the importance of their imagination, and how to fully use it?

The knowledge that we gain throughout our lifetime is either taught, or learned from watching others. For instance, it's very difficult to cook if you have never seen someone cook, or if you have not been taught. A baseball player can't be a good baseball player if he or she has never seen a baseball game played. If a person never saw what a baseball player does, he or she would be oblivious to what to do on a baseball field. If you want to be successful in anything, you have to know something about it. Seeing and being taught provides knowledge, and practice increases skill level and proficiency.

Many people do not know how to get what they want out of life. They can tell you they want wealth, love, happiness, and other things, but do not understand that those things can come to pass with help from our imagination. If you don't first imagination it and believe in it, it will never come to pass. Unfortunately, there are people that can tell you what they desire or desire to become, but don't know why they want it nor have a plan to make it a reality. Ask yourself, "Why do I desire this?" There's a good chance that you may get the desires of your heart, but then what?

One of the factors that often hinder what we imagine from coming true is our motive. Does what you desire benefit only you or can others benefit from it as well? Imagination is wonderful and can do outstanding things for our lives. However, what is birthed from our imagination should benefit others as well. We should not use our imaginations with selfish intentions, because this gift wasn't given to us to hoard, it was given to share. From the beginning, everything that God imagined and created wasn't only for Himself and Adam and Eve. It was also for their descendants, and all humanity.

Joel 2:28 says, "And it shall come to pass afterward, that I will pour out my spirit upon all flesh; and your sons and your daughters shall prophesy, your old men shall dream dreams, your young men shall see visions." In my opinion, Joel does a great job in illustrating the importance of a succession plan for our imagination. He quotes prophecy from our Heavenly Father.

One thing that we can probably agree on is that it is impossible to have a vision without a dream. To have *vision* means you have your sight set on something, or that you are anticipating something. Joel tells us that our old men will dream dreams, and our young men shall see visions. These old men were once young and more than likely had vision as young men, but now they are old and they have allowed their age to limit them, possibly because they are tired, or they are not physically able to accomplish what they once were. Perhaps this is why it is important that young men catch the vision regarding the dreams of old men.

On August 28, 1963, Martin Luther King, Jr. stood boldly on the steps of the Lincoln Memorial in

Washington D.C and passionately proclaimed that he had a dream. In front of over 250,000 people, with millions of others watching the speech on television or listening on radios, he shared his dream of freedom and equality. It's obvious that Martin Luther King Jr., knew his time on earth was coming to an end and that it would take others to accomplish his dream after his death. This is an example of how someone's dream can come to pass even after death, when others catch the vision. A succession plan for what we imagine is important.

This book is the succession plan of my imagination! One hundred years from now, when I am dead and gone, I want someone to pick up this book and testify of how it changed his or her life for the better. The word *succession* means; the coming of one person or thing after another in sequence. In other words, when a person's life or event comes to an end, there is another person or event that will replace the previous one and continue to move forward. The dream does not and should not end with them. Every life has an expiration date attached to it and everything that we've learned that is beneficial to the enhancement of another's life will be lost if we don't share it with someone.

While reading this book, I pray that something inside of you will ignite belief and confidence in what you can imagine. My prayer is that God will personally reveal something to you that will help you see your imagination in a brand new light. Hopefully you will gain new understanding of it, but more importantly, I hope you will actively use what God has revealed to you through imagination, to make your life more abundant. Many people do not believe the power of their imagination. Show them what has come out of yours and then teach them how to utilize their own gift of imagination by sharing what you've learned from the Word of God and from this book.

We do not know when we will take our last breath, but how much more comforting it will be knowing that when we leave this earth we also leave a succession plan for others. Now that's powerful!

8

Dream Versus Imagine

> "Imagination is everything. It is the preview of life's coming attractions."
> —Albert Einstein

In 2007, I was hired as the Program Coordinator for *Stop the Madness National, Inc.*, a non-profit organization founded by my father; Dr. Ternae Jordan, Sr. The mission of the organization is "to reduce the madness by touching lives and offering HOPE to youth, families and communities in an at-risk culture."

Over the years, I have worked with thousands of youth and their parents inspiring and encouraging them to "dream" big. Unfortunately, many adults and children struggle with the concept of dreaming. What happened to the dreamers? I honestly believe that if you don't have a dream, then you almost don't have a reason to live. God did not create us to be Robots; He created us to have life and to have it more abundantly.

God gave us His Son Jesus because He knows that Satan is stealing the gifts of dreaming and abundant life from His children. Again, Jesus says, *"The thief cometh not, but for to steal, and to kill, and to destroy: I come that they might have life, and that they might have it more abundantly"* (John 10:10, KJV). If this is what our Father desires for us and He has given us Jesus in order that we might live abundantly, then why do fewer and fewer people dream?

I believe that many people fail to dream simply because they lack imagination. This book is purposefully focused on *imagination*, and occasionally I reference the word *dream*. Understand that dreams and imagination are not synonymous, but are closely connected. They are almost identical in how they are formed in your mind. Now, I know this sounds like an oxymoron, but allow me to explain.

Dreams are *visual*, while imagination is an *action*. When you dream, it is either voluntary or involuntary vision of thoughts, images, or emotions. Dreams can be given to you. God can drop one in your spirit when you sleep, or you can create it in your mind. Imagination is the driving force to making that dream a reality. The two work together, but in order to exercise your imagination there has to be a dream or vision for which you strive.

I'll use cartoons as an example. Unlike many children today, I loved cartoons. Every Saturday morning I rushed to the television set with my bowl of cereal to watch cartoons like *Tom and Jerry*, *Bugs Bunny*, *He-Man*, *Daffy Duck*, *The Road Runner* and *The Smurfs*. When I got older and went to middle school, I rushed home after school everyday to watch *The Flintstones*. I was captivated by the colorful characters with charismatic personalities and I believe the cartoons actually enhanced my creativity and imagination as a child.

Unfortunately, when I ask elementary and middle school students today if they watch cartoons, they typically laugh and reply, "No, cartoons are for PUNKS!" I can't tell you how many times I've heard that from a child! Yet, I can only imagine the type of imagination that Charles-Emile Reynaud had when he created the very first projected animated cartoon film. Speaking of Charles Reynaud, I will use his creation of animated films as an example of how imagination and dreams work together.

In 1877, Charles-Emile Reynaud created a device called a "Praxinoscope" using the *"What If"* question we discussed in an earlier chapter. His invention was inspired by a device called the "Zoetrope." The zoetrope was simply a cylinder with vertical splits cut out around it that had various images in sequence drawn on a band on the inside of that cylinder. As the cylinder spins, you would look through the vertical splits and see the sequenced drawings give the illusion of movement when in actuality they were only still pictures.

Though the invention of the zoetrope was exciting, it did however have flaws. The biggest flaw that the device had was the moving image would appear blurry. So, Charles used the same concept, but replaced the vertical slits with mirrors in the middle of a cylinder, so that when the cylinder would spin you could see the reflection of those images in the mirrors which made the illusion of motion clearer, brighter, and without blur.

Although these two devices were creative and innovative, I am most impressed with the creation of each still picture, for without the imagination of the artist, those creative pictures could not be brought to life. You see, an animated cartoon artist imagines each picture he draws in great detail. The artist creates the moving object movement-by-movement, frame-by-frame, and he does so very carefully. After every picture is drawn, the artist aligns the pictures in the order they were created, then either by hand or mechanical device, flips through the aligned pages and watches each picture work together to create movement of that drawn object, thing, or cartoon character. Similarly, the same way an artist uses his imagination in detail to bring the images to life, so should we.

9

Commit To It

> "A dream doesn't become reality through magic; it takes sweat, determination and hard work."
> -Colin Powell

WOW! There I was staring at one of the most beautiful sights that my eyes have ever witnessed. I had always imagined it would happen but to experience it was totally different. As I stood there, my mind instantly played flashbacks of the numerous songs I had written about the occasion, the many heart breaks I had experienced, the many tuxedos I had worn for others who stood where I stood, and now it was finally my turn.

As soon as the flashbacks disappeared, my imagination began to take over as I stared at my beautiful bride to be. I found myself imagining and asking questions like, "What will my life be like from now on, will our friendship change after this day, and am I truly ready for this lifelong commitment?" It was

June 5, 2010 when she and I stood in front of hundreds of family and friends and vowed to take each other's hand in marriage. The occasion signified that we were making a vow to each other and to God that we would stay together until death.

WOW, talk about commitment! I was always told that when you make a vow to God—keep it. I knew that if our marriage was going to survive the test of time, my wife and I had to be committed to it. "Commitment" was a scary word. It was scary because it meant that regardless of whether things get difficult and I become weary and want to throw in the towel, I can't. It meant that when my bride-to-be became my wife, I had to throw away that little black book with all the phone numbers of women from my past. It meant that I had to be committed to one woman and that woman alone. I had to make up my mind whether I wanted to say, "I do," or "I don't." There was no in-between, and no straddling the fence. It was black or white, day or night, stay or go, yes or no. So as I stared at her and imagined the rest of my life with her, I said, "I certainly do!"

I have remained committed to Demetria Ann Jordan even when it was difficult; even when I wanted to walk away and give up, even when she and I were angry and didn't see eye to eye. Our commitment to God is what keeps us holding on. Our commitment to each other is what keeps our faith strong. Commitment is such a small word but has a huge meaning with gigantic results. In the depths of commitment lies success, good character, patience, growth, accomplishments, and so much more, but to get to those things you have to be committed until the end.

Commitment also means to work towards a goal until it is accomplished. What was the goal I had in mind when I said, "I certainly do" to my wife? It was to be with her until death. Like a married couple, we have to be so engaged with our imagination that if it no longer existed we would feel inadequate. We must trust, respect, protect, and love it. We must also be faithful to it.

When God created Adam and Eve, he gave them the command to "Be fruitful and multiply" (Gen 1:28). God commanded them to have children to subdue the earth. In other words, their children were to be so great in number that they would conquer this earth with authority and power. Our marriage to imagination should conceive and give birth to children named ideas, dreams, goals, and inventions. These children should subdue this entire earth to make it a better place and encourage others to subdue the earth in the same manner and to do so will require commitment.

Isn't it amazing how committed we are to things that don't really enhance our lives? Although we are supposed to be married to the imagination God created for us, we often find ourselves abandoning it. Oh yes we do! When we are more committed to working 9 to 5 at a job that was created through the imagination of another and let our dreams fall through the cracks, that's abandonment. There is nothing wrong with assisting another's imagination to prosper. That's what we do when we work a job, but we can't lose sight of our commitment to our own dreams and what we imagine for ourselves. Those of us committed to 9 to 5's have to remind ourselves that these companies are only "renting" our time. When we clock out, we have to go home to our imagination that needs the same, or if not more attention than we give to other things.

If it's not the job, maybe it's in front of the television where many people spend 80 percent of their lives' watching sitcoms, reality shows, movies, and sports birthed through the imagination of someone else, while that someone else becomes wealthy from our viewing pleasures. All too often we fall asleep in front of a television only to wake the next morning and head off to that same 9 to 5 that barely helps us make ends meet. Please, don't misconstrue what I'm saying. There is absolutely nothing wrong with working our jobs; however, we should never be so committed to our jobs that we lose sight of our own desires. God created imagination in us from birth, which means it was meant for us to have and use for God's Glory.

If you are guilty of not being committed to your imagination and sincerely want to be, I have a simple solution for you–REPENT! It's that simple. I did it and highly recommend you do so too. To *repent* means to "turn from." Acknowledge to God that you have fallen short of His expectations for you, seek His forgiveness for your negligence, and

NEVER DO IT AGAIN! Then take the next step—forgive yourself.

In June of 2013, I accepted the position of Assistant Pastor at the Mt. Canaan Baptist Church in Chattanooga, TN, where my grandfather Emeritus Melvin Jordan, pastored for 40 years. After he retired from pastoring he passed the torch on to my father, Dr. Ternae Jordan, Sr., who is currently carrying on the legacy. As a child of a pastor I've always been active in church ministry, but never desired to be a pastor of a church. I've been traumatized by what I have witnessed in the life of a pastor when dealing with people in the church, and I vowed never to have parts in that ministry. So imagine my surprise when God laid it on my heart to become an Assistant Pastor. Come on, that's just like being a "pastor." What? Lord, are you serious? What's the difference? I mean, I did accept my call to be a minister, but an assistant pastor totally caught me off guard. People often ask me, if I was so against being an assistant pastor, then why did I accept the position. Well, it's like this. God speaks to people in various ways. The way I know God is speaking to me and calling me to do something is when my flesh says no, but my spirit says yes. I definitely fought this idea of assistant pastoring, but when I saw my pastor and father getting hurt and burnt by people he considered friends, daughters and sons in the ministry, my spirit stood up and I heard God say, "help your father with the vision, I've given him." When I heard God in my spirit say this, I humbly accepted. Was I reluctant? Absolutely! But when God calls you to something, it is in your best interest to say, "Yes Lord." I must admit though, there have been many times that I've cried in this job because I felt like God had forgotten about the vision He has given me. I often feel as if I give 90% to other people's vision, and invest only 10% to my own. Miraclechild Media Group, Inc., is the vision God has given me, and the vision was given to me while at church during my sophomore year in college.

One Sunday morning, I woke up exhausted from a long night of partying with my fraternity brothers, it was our week of events on campus, and we ended the successful week with a party. Oh, how I was dreading to get out of that bed to go to anybody's church that morning. Nevertheless, somehow I found enough energy and strength to make it to service. As soon as I arrived into the doors of the church, lack of sleep and exhaustion attacked me. "Oh no, this is going to be a long service", I thought to myself. However, I am so glad that I fought through it, because God was not only going to bless me through the service, but He was going to cast vision into my heart. About forty-five minutes into the service, I closed my eyes and right between sleep and reality I saw a vision. Have you ever seen a television that was recently turned off, and on the screen you saw the silhouette of previous images still on the screen? Well, that's what I saw in my vision, however, the screen that I saw was a movie screen. Silhouettes on a blank movie screen captured me, while everything around me was dark, but within the darkness I heard people crying, worshiping, and praising God. I don't know what was previous on that screen, but obviously it was something that provoked the presence of God in the atmosphere, where chains were broken, hearts were changed, deliverance occurred, and my call was established. It was there at that moment when God said to me, "T.J., I want you to use film, music, and other forms of media to encourage those of the faith and lead people who do not know me, to me." There, right

on that church pew in the midst of shouts of praise
and worship is where I answered that call.

This may sound crazy, but one of my frustrations in
life is that I've been blessed with many gifts and tal-
ents, and though that may seem great, it is actually
bittersweet. I have many friends who are extremely
successful doing one thing. Rather its music, film,
law, pastoring, or teaching, they love that one thing
and have gone all out perfecting that one thing
and are living their dream. As for me, I love EN-
TERTAINMENT! I am a recording artist, singer,
songwriter, actor, author, videographer, video editor,
speaker, preacher, teacher, scriptwriter, producer,
and more. My biggest concern and sometimes fear
is to become a jack-of-all-trades and a master of
nothing. In my frustration, I have often asked God,
"What do you want from me?" What do you want
me to do? However, I must be honest and say I was
scared to hear His answer. I've always been told to be
careful what you ask for, because you just might get
it. Therefore, after much prayer and fasting, waiting
and seeking, God finally answered my question. To
my surprise, He said, I want you to do everything,
but do it under the umbrella of your testimony and

miracle, and this is how Miraclechild Media Group, Inc., was birthed and established. Miraclechild Media Group, Inc.'s mission is *"to provide high quality forms of media that will encourage, inspire, uplift and motivate the lives of our customers. We aim to become an international recognized faith-based company. We view ourselves as trendsetters in an industry plagued with negative forms of media. Through music, books, films, and other forms of entertainment we aspire to help people see the potential for their lives, strengthen their faith and fulfill their purpose."*

I said all of this to say; I've asked God, why do you have me in an assistant pastor position, working someone else's vision, when you've given me a vision of my own?   It wasn't until one day I was meeting with the various ministry leaders in the church when He gave me the answer to that question. He said, "How are you going to manage and run an empire like Miraclechild Media Group, with all of its entities, if you can't manage the ministries that you presently oversee?" Wow, talking about a slap in the face, this answer was definitely a wake up call. God is saying to us all, if we stay committed to where He has us now, stay faithful, do our job with excellence;

we will be ready and prepared for what He has for us. *"His master replied, well done, good and faithful servant! You have been faithful with a few things; I will put you in charge of many things. Come and share your master's happiness (Matthew 25:21, NIV).*

There have been many times I felt like my dreams have slipped through my fingers and I thought I saw my dreams and vision pass me by. I thought to myself, "Dude, you're getting older, and now it's too late give up, be content, and be happy with where you are." Then God had to say to me, "TJ, Shut up! All you need to do is stay committed to where I have you now, stay committed to your dreams, continue to complete projects one at time and when I'm ready to release what I've promised to you, you'll be ready!"

So, this book is one of many projects that I have completed. I really thank you for investing in this book; by doing so, you are investing in the vision of Miraclechild Media Group, and God's Kingdom. I can't wait to share with you what has already been completed! We are just waiting on God! When He is ready to release them to the world, we will be ready! Stay tuned!

10

Prove And Appreciate

> "Imagination should not be used to escape reality, but to create It."
>
> –Colin Wilson

I prayed, waited and imagined this day. It was Friday, February 1, 2013. I was extremely exhausted from anticipation, excited about what was about to happen and nervous at the same time. "Is this really happening?" I asked myself. I knew it would happen one day because by faith I believed it would. However, it still felt like it should be a few years away, but to actually be witnessing it at that very moment was surreal. It wasn't until the doctor looked at my wife and said, "Are you ready" that reality kicked in that this was the real deal.

As I looked at my wife lying on the hospital bed sweating from pain and exhaustion, I immediately knew within the next few moments our lives would never be the same. After all of the scenarios we had created through conversation, the prayers we had prayed together, the pictures we had imagined regarding the birth of our first child, the time had finally arrived and the imagery was now about to become a reality. "Oh no, am I ready for this?" "What kind of father will I be?" "How will the dynamics of our marriage change?" "Whom would our baby look like?" All of these questions began to run through my mind, along with degrees of faith, fear and doubt. It may sound crazy, but before the nurse asked, "Are you ready?" I really was perfectly fine. I did not remotely resemble those fathers we had laughed at on *YouTube* videos. You know, the ones who faint while watching their wives give birth, or those who finally realize that the birth process is extremely grotesque and messy, and in terror, they run out of the room. Oh NO, not me! I was among the men who saw their lives flash before their eyes, who were concerned about what was next.

I was that man who saw his dreams and what he imagined finally coming true but wasn't sure if he was asking for too much too fast. I suddenly got nervous. Embarrassing emotions seemed to torture me internally, yet I found both courage and strength to encourage my wife as she pushed our little bundle of joy, the one we prayed, fasted, imagined, and waited for into this world. We had waited for this moment far longer than our 3 am arrival at the hospital. We had waited since we said, "I do" at the altar. This was our moment.

As my wife pushed, I watched with amazement her strength and determination to deliver our blessing. "Oh my goodness", I said to myself. "I am about to become a father." As I began to get a glimpse of our daughter's head, the feelings of negativity and doubt no longer existed. My heart began to beat faster, tears began to fill my eyes, and a smirk appeared on my face. "This is it," I thought!

We had waited in the hospital eleven hours. It was 2:26 p.m. when my wife made the final push. Out came our 7lbs. and 1oz. baby girl, Deanna Katrina Jordan. My mother and mother-in-law both witnessed with us the birth of their first granddaughter. What we had imagined was now a reality. By the way, remember in a previous chapter I told you that I gave my wife a Mother's Day card before we knew she was pregnant and I signed the card with names of our imaginary children? Well, my wife informed me recently that I didn't sign the card with both children's names. I signed it with only "Deanna's" name. Wow, now that's amazing!

The reason I chose to share this moment with you is because I want to share "living proof" that God will *birth* promises out of imagination. I had imagined my daughter's existence before she was ever conceived. She is alive and healthy. There may be things that you have imagined for your life, and you are in the birthing stage of it coming into pass. You see the head of it coming, but suddenly you aren't so sure if you are ready for it. You feel unprepared, undeserving, and fear is beginning to take over. It's okay, it happens to the best of us. It happened to me.

There is a wonderful and powerful quote by Franklin D. Roosevelt that reads: "We have nothing to fear, but fear itself." Fear is tricky and deceitful. Fear wants to keep us stagnant and away from the promises and will of God. The only way to fight fear is to accomplish what fear is keeping you from accomplishing. Do what fear is deterring you from doing. Go where fear does not want you to go. That's how you fight fear. Beat it at it's own game. Ignore it and move forward with your plans—not fear's plans.

God proved that He would honor my dreams and imaginations. The birth of Deanna is an example. Yes, I found fear internally for a moment, but I had to reassure myself that God would not have allowed my imagination of her birth to become a reality if I was not prepared. God said that he would give us provision for our vision. We have to know that if what we imagine is coming true, we are prepared. We were prepared when we envisioned it. I was prepared to be a father when I prayed for my daughter to be created. When I first imagined writing this book, I was prepared to finish it, and now you are reading the final chapter.

As you near completion of reading this book, I have a few questions for you to consider: What are you going to do with the information you've gained or have been reminded of? How are you going to show your appreciation to God for allowing it to become reality?

There have been hundreds of dreams that I have imagined that God has brought to pass. He knew that I would do right by each dream and use each dream for His glory. I don't know what you have imagined or are imagining right now for your life, but I hope that this book has inspired and encouraged you to imagine the unimaginable, to believe the unbelievable and to tap into your child-like imagination.

Lastly, I want to remind you of the entire basis of this book. We are made in the image of God and in His likeness. If God can imagine something, and speak it into existence, then we can too! God gave us this gift and we have a responsibility to use it to make the world a better place. Through it we can give God glory. This is the ultimate "Thank You" we can give Him. Let's do it—you and I!

Epilogue

I was only 15 years old at the time of that fateful event that changed my life forever. One minute I was preparing for a dream that I had imagined for most of my short life, and the next moment I awoke in the hospital, blind. I could not have imagined that a stray bullet lodging in my head almost altered my dreams.

Maybe you've never experienced physical blindness, but you have experienced blindness as it relates to your dreams. You imagined what your dream looked like, you could see it vividly, but then suddenly you lost sight of it.

Perhaps you've never been threatened with brain damage or any life altering situations; however, your imagination and the vision and dreams once had, have been damaged or altered. Maybe you've experienced difficulty making good decisions and you find yourself feeling crippled in your ability to take the right steps to accomplish your dreams. These are things that I've experienced both physically and psychologically. However, the same God that miraculously healed me from blindness, possible brain damage, and being crippled can and will (according to His will) restore your imagination.

This book is my testimony. What's yours?

CPSIA information can be obtained
at www.ICGtesting.com
Printed in the USA
LVHW010427121220
673985LV00002B/3

9 780692 451126